D0880938

Great Jobs in Technology

Tom Streissguth

ReferencePoint Press®

San Diego, CA

About the Author

Tom Streissguth has authored more than one hundred books in many different subjects, including geography, history, biography, sports, and current events. He attended Yale University, where he majored in music, and has worked as a teacher, editor, and journalist. In 2015 he founded the Archive (www.historicjournalism.com), an online collection of historic journalism, as a resource for students, educators, and researchers. Under its imprint, he is publishing a series of journalism collections for the school and library market.

© 2019 ReferencePoint Press, Inc.
Printed in the United States

For more information, contact:
ReferencePoint Press, Inc.
PO Box 27779
San Diego, CA 92198
www.ReferencePointPress.com

Picture Credits:

Cover: Gorodenkoff/Shutterstock.com
 6: Maury Aaseng
21: iStockphoto.com
36: Ton Koene/agefotostock/Newsom
45: dotshock/Shutterstock.com
69: gilaxia/iStockphoto.com

LIBRARY OF CONGRESS CATALOGING-IN-PUBLICATION DATA

Name: Streissguth, Thomas, 1958– author.
Title: Great Jobs in Technology/by Tom Streissguth.
Description: San Diego, CA: ReferencePoint Press, Inc., [2019] | Series:
  Great Jobs | Audience: Grade 9 to 12. | Includes bibliographical
  references and index.
Identifiers: LCCN 2018034086 (print) | LCCN 2018038667 (ebook) | ISBN
  9781682825303 (eBook) | ISBN 9781682825297 (hardback)
Subjects: LCSH: Technology—Vocational guidance—Juvenile literature. |
  Computer programming--Vocational guidance—Juvenile literature. | Computer
  science—Vocational guidance—Juvenile literature. | Computer
  industry—Employment—Juvenile literature.
Classification: LCC T65.3 (ebook) | LCC T65.3 .S77 2019 (print) | DDC
  602.3—dc23
LC record available at https://lccn.loc.gov/2018034086

Contents

Introduction: A Market for Smart,
Creative People   4

Data Security Analyst   8

Data Architect   16

Roboticist   24

Game Developer   32

Mobile Developer   40

User Experience Designer   48

Artificial Intelligence Specialist   56

Website Developer   64

Interview with a Roboticist   73

Other Jobs in Technology   76

Index   77

A Market for Smart, Creative People

The room fills with the buzz of conversation and the busy clacking of laptop keys. Groups of people sit around the tables, bouncing their ideas back and forth, arguing about network environments, augmented reality (AR) and virtual reality, visual application programming interfaces, scalability, and code. Every corner of the room has tech geeks talking, explaining, and dreaming up crazy, cool stuff that will probably never become reality.

This is a hackathon, where those assembled have twenty-four hours to solve a problem with a useful, usable app. This one runs every year in Austin, Texas, at the South By Southwest music festival—always texted as *SXSW*. Coders, programmers, and hackers gather in a large room to create and test under serious deadline pressure. At the end, a panel of judges declares a winner. Prize money is paid for the best ideas.

A Competition for Talent

Naturally, any hackathon at SXSW welcomes music apps. The 2017 winners in the music category were Paul Wehner and Tom Bruckner, who partnered on an AR program for musicians to use in studio and for live performance. Afterwards, they wrote up a business plan, then formed a start-up in Los Angeles—the center of the music and entertainment world.

In a short time, Wehner and Bruckner had a beta version of their AR music platform ready for a test run. Music producer David Block, who created The Human Experience performance project, brought their concept to the live stage. "The support and contacts from the SXSW Hackathon and subsequent incubation program have given us a turbo boost towards our mission of unlocking the creativity of beginner and professional musicians with AR," Wehner and Bruckner told an SXSW blogger.

The SXSW Hackathon inspires a lot of start-ups, but it also has major corporate backing. Amazon Web Services, the digital hacker magazine *Hacker Noon,* the Capitol Music Group, and Consensys, a global tech and development company, are all on board as partners or sponsors. These companies actively recruit at SXSW and many other venues, including job fairs, conferences, conventions, and seminars. They are searching and competing for good tech talent, and they have a lot of jobs open to qualified applicants.

A Hot Market for Techs

It is a good time to be a tech geek. The variety of tech jobs is increasing as far-out science fiction concepts such as AR, private rocketry, and industrial robotics go commercial. New tech companies are starting up constantly, offering good pay and the chance for quick advancement. Chief executive officers of big, established companies are looking for smart, creative people to bring apps to market, manage their data, build their machines, and program their devices.

There is no limit to the possibilities—technology reaches almost every corner of life and business. Just as the SXSW Hackathon is open to all ages and ability levels, the tech world is open to newcomers with nothing more than ideas to share and develop. "I got the initial phone call because I'd worked on an open source project with an employee who referred me," explains Eevee, a programmer, on the popular site Vox. "I got my previous job based on a Pokemon fansite I started when I was 12!"

Experience counts, of course, as does education and demonstrated skills and knowledge. Equally important are creative-thinking skills and the ability to see how apps and platforms can

Great Jobs in Technology

Occupation	Minimum Educational Requirements	2017 Median Pay
Computer and information systems manager	Bachelor's degree	$139,220
Computer hardware engineer	Bachelor's degree	$115,120
Computer network architect	Bachelor's degree	$104,650
Computer support specialist	Associate's degree	$52,810
Computer systems analyst	Bachelor's degree	$88,270
Database administrator	Bachelor's degree	$87,020
Electrical and electronics engineer	Bachelor's degree	$97,970
Information security analyst	Bachelor's degree	$95,510
Network and computer systems administrator	Bachelor's degree	$81,100
Software developer	Bachelor's degree	$103,560
Web developer	High school diploma or equivalent	$67,990

Source: Bureau of Labor Statistics, *Occupational Outlook Handbook*, 2018. www.bls.gov.

work to meet a need or solve a problem. Tech skills apply in every sector of the economy, and they are needed by for-profit, non-profit, and public sector organizations. That means a great job in tech can also be a job in media, health care, retail, or the hospitality industry—in whatever direction an applicant's interest or passion lies.

Climbing the Ladder of Opportunity

At most jobs, a tech worker will also find a long ladder of opportunity waiting to be climbed. Because this kind of knowledge is valuable, it can bring an employee to management levels quickly. It also opens up other opportunities; for example, it is common for certain tech jobs, such as those in data security, to be in demand in many locations, among many different employers. Many tech jobs are open to freelancers, who are consultants who work on their own time and their own schedule. And for those with an interest in running things, smart innovations bring the chance to build a start-up company that creates its own profitable niche in the tech universe.

It is not necessary to be a genius hacker, or to win a hackathon, to get a start in tech. Anyone interested can take a few classes, try a summer camp or internship, or just volunteer to help a nonprofit that needs a hand in collecting data or building a web page. As opportunities present themselves, newbies in this field will discover soon enough what is boring and what is interesting, and they can apply effort and time in the right direction. There seems to be no limit to the future possibilities of computers, robots, artificial intelligence, and those who work in the many cool corners of technology.

Data Security Analyst

At a Glance

Data Security Analyst

Minimum Educational Requirements
A bachelor's degree in computer science, data science, mathematics, software design, or other information technology subjects

Personal Qualities
Communication and problem-solving skills; patience; thoroughness; team player; interest in new technologies

Certification and Licensing
Licensing is not required; certification is available but not required

Working Conditions
Indoors, working on computers or monitoring systems in control rooms; on the road as a consultant or installer of security systems

Salary Range
From $55,560 to $153,090 annually

Number of Jobs
100,000 in 2016

Future Job Outlook
Predicted growth of 28 percent through 2026, which is faster than average

What Does a Data Security Analyst Do?

There are a lot of sharks swimming in the waters of technology, networks, and the Internet. They are hungry for data—very important, private data such as Social Security numbers, bank account passwords, and private e-mails—that they can use to gain access to someone's money. Or they are phishing for weapons blueprints, planning documents, or encrypted messages that can reveal the intentions of an opponent on the battlefield or of a law enforcement agency trying to stop a terrorist strike.

According to an IBM study on data breaches in 2017, the average cost of a single data breach was $3.62 million. The average size of these breaches was more than twenty-four thousand records. For that reason, companies and government agencies will pay

8

a lot of money for data security analysts (DSAs) who can stop the attacks and secure vital information.

DSAs guard against cyberattacks, hacking, phishing operations that seek out private data, and so-called greenmail, which is a variant of blackmail in which a hacker steals confidential business info and demands money for keeping it secret. A security analyst must find vulnerable points where an outsider might breach a system with a stolen password, a phishing e-mail, or a malware program installed remotely or on-site. Any company that communicates information over the Internet or other data networks is a target—and needs its data protected.

A DSA knows how protective computer firewalls work and understands encryption technology, which is the science of hiding data by rendering it into alphanumeric codes to which only key holders have access. Security analysts perform regular security audits, train employees and users in security procedures, set up policies, and manage passwords and access levels. To break into the field, analysts "need to decide what to specialize in," reports Roger Grimes in a CSO Online Security Adviser column. "The computer security field is huge and covers dozens of disciplines including firewalls, IDS [intrusion detection system], SIEM [security information and event management], security assessment, host hardening, and patching." These systems and techniques provide data networks with a protective layer to guard against cyberattacks.

DSAs who work in security operations centers (SOCs) spend their days in front of computer monitors or wall screens in large control rooms, directing traffic through a network and dealing with a constant stream of threats. "We never know what is going to happen," comments Jim Treinen, a security analyst for Protect-Wise, a network security firm. "A day can start out calm or start out on fire and very quickly go from one or another."

On arrival, the prior shift updates the DSA on the system's status and any incidents that may have occurred. Tough decisions must be made; it is not a job for robots or software alone.

In a YouTube interview, Richard Cassidy of the data security firm Alert Logic explains that "when they sit at the desk, the first thing our SOC analyst will do is look at the open cases. They've got very strict SLAs [service-level agreements] by which they have to respond to our customers and ensure that they review all of the data in intrinsic detail to make the right decision. Because what we don't want to do here . . . is to rely on an automated system."

DSAs spend a lot of time learning and using security software. They use these programs to detect outside intrusions and track down their source. They also recommend new procedures to enhance a company's systems security. This means teaching employees—one-on-one or in a group setting—how to manage their devices and computers to protect against data breaches.

Spending on cybersecurity reached $86.4 billion in 2017, when it was growing at the rate of 7 percent every year. According to St. Mary's University, a Minnesota school that offers a two-year master of science degree in cybersecurity, there will be 2 million unfilled cybersecurity jobs by 2020, meaning there is a serious shortage of skilled workers in this area.

Despite the shortage, becoming a successful DSA is not easy. The learning curve is steep in this field, and applicants must show they're keeping up with the constant changes and innovations. Certifications are how applicants for data security jobs show potential employers their level of experience and professionalism. Staying current and demonstrating such knowledge in the field is the best way to acquire and keep a data security job.

How Do You Become a Data Security Analyst?

Education

At most companies, DSAs must hold a college degree in a computer-related field. Some employers may require advanced degrees, including a master of science in cybersecurity. Education in this field is an ongoing process. There are cybersecurity academies that train professionals in the latest developments. The Cyber Security Academy in Monroe, Washington, offers several different courses, including training for certified ethical hacking, which is the practice of finding the weak spots of a system by attempting to hack into it.

Certification and Licensing

Licensing of DSAs is not required by any state or federal agencies, but many analysts pursue them to show the scope of their knowledge. Important certifications in the field include the systems security certified practitioner, the SANS Institute certificates, the certified information systems security professional (CISSP), and the certified information security manager. The CISSP certification, for instance, requires five years of professional experience, but candidates may substitute a year of relevant education or another approved credential.

Everybody in the field has an opinion on the merits of these certifications, many of which come with their own specialized classes, instructors, books, and practice examinations. The SANS Institute, for example, is one of several trusted companies that offer courses in the network defense, digital forensics, and other security measures. Grimes remarks, "If I see that someone has a SANS certification, then I know they're on top of their stuff."

Volunteer Work and Internships

Volunteers are welcome at many organizations to assist with data security. Smaller companies, start-ups, schools, and nonprofits may not have the budget to hire an outside security consultant or a paid staff member to do the job. In return for managing their data or tutoring their staffs in best practices, these organizations offer volunteers the experience of applying their systems and communication skills in a real-world situation.

Internships in data security are offered by consulting firms as well as private and public companies and government agencies at the state and federal level. The Central Intelligence Agency, for example, posts a paid internship in which undergraduates assist cybersecurity officers in the work of analyzing, auditing, and upgrading agency defenses against outside intrusion. The US Department of Homeland Security offers the Cyber Student Volunteer Initiative, a summer internship program in which graduate and undergraduate students are guided in work projects and are mentored by cybersecurity experts.

Skills and Personality

DSAs need excellent problem-solving skills to contend with the many ways in which hackers seek to enter systems. They need the persistence to address and resolve problems, challenges, and breaches, and they need to be detail-oriented because they watch over large amounts of system performance data to detect any changes that might reveal a cyberattack in progress. They also must have the patience to serve as educators for users who may not be familiar with security software or be aware of the risks to their own systems.

On the Job

Employers

DSAs work for private businesses, government agencies, and nonprofit sectors such as education. Many work for companies that design computer operating systems. Software firms and computer manufacturers hire full-time, permanent security analysts to protect their products from the threat of intrusion. Other analysts are employed by financial and insurance firms that require high-level security systems—and analysts to administer them—to prevent the loss of customer data.

DSAs working as consultants—whether independently or as part of a consulting firm—are hired by clients in private business, government, education, and other fields. Their assignments might last a few weeks to several years. They ensure that data, passwords, communications such as e-mails, and other sensitive materials are kept secure from stealing, hacking, snooping, or other misuse.

Working Conditions

DSAs work indoors on computer systems to constantly monitor traffic and data access. For many, this is a full-time job. Some are on call 24/7 in case of threats, breaches, or cyberattacks. To respond to a breach, they may have to work overtime to identify the source, patch the vulnerabilities in the system, and come up with a method to prevent future intrusions. The pressure to secure data in the event of a cyberattack can be intense—the big retailer Target and the credit-reporting company Equifax both lost billions of dollars after cyberattacks stole sensitive client and customer data.

Earnings

According to the Bureau of Labor Statistics, the annual median salary for DSAs reached $95,510 as of 2017. The high end of the scale reached $153,090 per year, and the lowest salaries started at $55,560. Profit sharing, bonuses, and stock options may also boost the annual income for employees at larger, more successful companies.

Opportunities for Advancement

With experience, DSAs can move into supervisory or management roles. Some decide to break away from regular employment to work on a freelance basis for their own clients. They can also move into related jobs, such as network administrator. Experienced DSAs have much to offer software companies seeking to get the latest security features into their apps. Specializing in new software and applications offers a path to a good job as a software engineer or mobile developer. And with the importance of cyberwarfare increasing all the time, a security analyst can also move from the private sector to governments, both foreign and domestic, to protect data critical to military functions, voting, public health records, financial and tax functions, and education.

What Is the Future Outlook for Data Security Analysts?

As digital systems pervade every aspect of business and people's lives, the need to protect systems against malicious intrusion grows. Medical and financial records, retail transactions, and government databases are all vulnerable to hackers seeking to use the information for financial gain. DSAs are also fighting on the front lines of a global information war in which nations attack and disrupt military operations, utility grids, election systems, and vital infrastructure such as airports, dams, and power plants. This means the demand for skilled security techs for a wide variety of organizations, and all over the world, will continue to grow.

Find Out More

Federal Trade Commission (FTC)
600 Pennsylvania Ave. NW
Washington, DC 20580
website: www.ftc.gov

The FTC offers a webpage with up-to-date information on the data security front. It includes tips for app developers on best security practices, the fight against identity theft and ransomware, news on major breaches at companies such as Uber and Equifax, and a guide to the rules the FTC enforces on health security, credit bureaus, and telecommunications providers.

KrebsonSecurity
website: https://krebsonsecurity.com

A former cybersecurity reporter for the *Washington Post*, Brian Krebs produces this blog on cybersecurity and cybercrime, giving updates on the activities of various groups of hackers, phishers, and malware and ransomware perpetrators. This is a great place to learn about the many evolving varieties of cybercrime.

Wombat Security Blog

website: www.wombatsecurity.com/blog

This blog features news and updates on developments in the cybersecurity field and security threats such as e-mail phishing and data breaches. This is a good place to get a feel for the kind of work and information that data security experts deal with every day.

Woz U

website: https://woz-u.com

Started by Apple cofounder Steve Wozniak, Woz U offers an online cybersecurity program that introduces users to the fundamentals of the science through high-definition video instruction, one-on-one mentors, and browser-based labs. Geared toward recent graduates, the course requires some knowledge of systems and networks.

Data Architect

Data Architect

Minimum Educational Requirements
Bachelor's degree in computer or information science, with some knowledge of key database languages

Personal Qualities
Strong analytical sense; computer aptitude; ability to communicate with clients and colleagues; attention to detail; math skills; problem-solving ability

Certification and Licensing
Licensing is not required; certification is sometimes required

Working Conditions
Indoors, working on laptops and desktop systems; consultants often travel to various work sites on temporary assignments

Salary Range
From $79,000 to $160,000 annually

Number of Jobs
287,000 in 2016

Future Job Outlook
Predicted growth rate of 11 percent through 2026, which is faster than average

What Does a Data Architect Do?

Data is the lifeblood of business, government, education, and health care. Nearly every organization that provides goods or services compiles and utilizes data. There is so much data available that more than a quarter of a million people are employed just to organize it. Some of those individuals who put data into logical structures are called data architects.

Data architects are responsible for building systems that hold data. Their job is to set up these systems so that people without any special technical skill can use them. Doctors, for example, now pull up electronic medical records whenever a patient comes for an office visit. Bank tellers access account information to take deposits from customers. Companies such as Amazon and Google need data on their users to market their services and target advertising. Data science can be useful to law enforcement officers, who monitor traffic on the web to root out criminal enterprises such as drug trafficking or money laundering. Data architects are responsible for making these tasks possible and easy.

Data architects primarily keep data systems running on physical servers or in the so-called cloud, which is a method of storing information off-site in the vast, interconnected storage spaces of the Internet. Data architects prepare backups to keep the data safe in case of a system crash or hacking attempt. They maintain metadata registries, which are indexes that describe the types of data stored. They also serve as enforcers, ensuring that data is brought into the system in a consistent manner and format.

It is a challenging, rewarding job with a bright future. Tech author John Parkinson insists on his LinkedIn page that "data architecture is exciting." He explains that "information weaves and flows around the organization. It ducks and dives, it merges and splits, some stays where it's put and some never stays still. . . . And all the time, every second of every day, people and machines use it to make decisions. . . . Taming and controlling information flow so that the right information gets to the right people at the right time—what a great job."

Data architects build new databases when a company decides to expand into a different business sector or target a foreign market. This can be a huge job. Creating a database means modeling, building, and implementing the system and then setting up new user interfaces for colleagues. It also entails setting the rules for who will control the data, who will be allowed to access it, and how it will be kept safe.

To carry out these duties, data architects use many software languages and a wide range of database applications. They have to be fluent in SQL, a database language used by companies of all sizes and in many different business sectors. Advanced programs, such as Apache Hadoop or Azure SQL, a cloud storage system from Microsoft, set up the data warehouses where information is stored.

Data architects use these tools to solve tough, complex puzzles using logic, math, intuition, and experience. In an interview on the website Knowledgent, big data architect Dip Kharod says, "I love addressing the challenges presented by the massive amount of data being generated every day. Implementing new solutions for clients is the best part of the job! Big Data is a huge field, and it's natural to get lost with so many new tools and technologies. So my suggestion would be to grab the first opportunity that you get. Press on and more opportunities will follow."

Data architects may also seek open-source solutions, meaning they can get suggestions from outside the business or even from the public on how to organize information. Even federal agencies that need to keep much of their data classified may turn to open-source solutions not only to solve their data issues but also to recruit new employees. Chris Mattmann, the principal data scientist at NASA's Jet Propulsion Laboratory (JPL), explains in an interview on the *Master's in Data Science Blog* that "being involved with open source has provided an amazing recruitment tool since we can share our problems with the broader community and work together with those outside NASA on solutions to our software problems that are open source. This allows us to battle test our potential talent and give them real problems to work with to see if JPL is a place they'd like to work."

How Do You Become a Data Architect?

Education

Data architects need a bachelor's degree in computer science or a related field. Advanced degrees prepare students for jobs at higher management levels. Many colleges and universities offer degree programs in the data management field. Hands-on experience in programming is essential. Data architects must know how systems are built, from the building blocks of code to the design of the user interface. They also should know something about the business sector in which they hope to work. "I would much rather have a very mediocre data scientist who really understood the business than the reverse," Jeffrey McMillan, chief data officer of the multinational bank Morgan Stanley, says on the data security training website Cybrary. "Because the reverse doesn't help me at all. It's not about the algorithm. It's about understanding of the business."

Certification and Licensing

Licensing is not required in this field, but some employers may require certification from job applicants. The key certification for data architects is the certified data management professional (CDMP). The CDMP recognizes four levels of expertise: associate, practitioner, master, and fellow. The associate level requires at least six months of relevant work experience, a bachelor's degree, and a passing score on the CDMP examination. The highest level, fellow, requires more than twenty years of experience as well as expert knowledge. Many fellow candidates have also published blogs or articles and have made original contributions to the body of knowledge in data science.

The Institute for the Certification of Computing Professionals offers CDMP exams at test centers throughout the country. Once a candidate attains the certification, it must be renewed every three years by completing at least 120 hours of continuing education.

Volunteer Work and Internships

Volunteering as a data architect poses creative challenges that can hone the skills of students and starters in the field. Several organizations harness the power of data analysis for nonprofit groups and charitable causes. Volunteers submit proposals to meet the needs of the group or cause. The goal is to adapt the work of statistical modeling and advanced algorithms to help battle hunger, for example, or research the world's mountain of health statistics to find regions that may need medical assistance to stop a rampant disease. Donating time and experience can be rewarding and offer data architects new fields to explore.

Taking an internship is also a good way to explore new opportunities. For example, an internship allows candidates to learn the specific needs of large companies that are hiring. It is also a way for a student to audition a company, learn about its culture and mission, and develop marketable skills. Especially relevant specialties for interns include application architecture, network management, and system performance management. For many interns, a few weeks spent toiling at a low-level task has opened doors for full-time and well-paid positions.

Skills and Personality

Data architects need analytical and problem-solving talent, communication skills, and the ability to work in teams. Also helpful are patience, persistence, and the mental stamina to handle complex, multilevel projects. In their work with nonexpert colleagues, data analysts need a sense of empathy and the ability to render technical jargon in plain English. They also must have a sense of responsibility for a company's or client's data security because they are entrusted with sensitive—sometimes classified or confidential—information. The pressure of deadlines is a constant companion, as many of the problems in this field are time-sensitive, and system crashes and glitches can also complicate the workday.

On the Job

Employers

Businesses of all sizes hire data architects to handle their information systems. The Census Bureau, a federal agency, needs them to organize the count of US residents that takes place every ten years. Universities handle reams of data on their student population and new applicants. Hospitals and clinics collect and organize massive databases on their patients and workers. These employers need applicants with skills in database design, development, management, modeling, and warehousing. The road to better-paid positions as a data architect begins with programming or database administration.

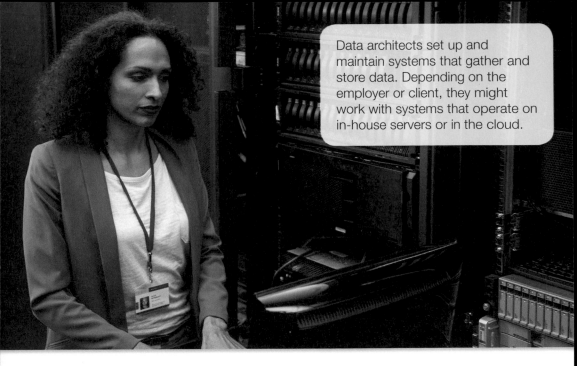

Data architects set up and maintain systems that gather and store data. Depending on the employer or client, they might work with systems that operate on in-house servers or in the cloud.

Working Conditions

It is common for data architects to spend most of their time working indoors on laptop and desktop computer systems. They communicate via phone and e-mail with colleagues and clients, and they attend meetings—often in the form of conference calls over the Internet—to coordinate their work with other team members. They work under project deadlines and put in overtime when needed. Data architects who work independently as consultants put in a lot of travel time visiting clients in distant locales to advise on project status.

Earnings

According to the Bureau of Labor Statistics, the median pay for what it terms *computer systems analysts* reached $88,230 per year in 2017. The agency does not break down figures for data architects, but several large job websites with data of their own do provide this information. PayScale reports that the average pay for a data architect is $151,734; Glassdoor lists the average salary for a senior data architect as $121,693. CareerBuilder pegged the average annual salary for data architects in 2018 at $110,000, with a wide range between $79,000 and $160,000.

As with any job in tech and other fields, salaries vary according to responsibilities, experience, and the employer's location.

Opportunities for Advancement

A data architect can move into more senior levels of a company, working as an information manager or project lead. Since handling data has become such a major part of business operations, an expert in this field has a path to executive-level positions such as chief information officer. Also, a data architect may advance in a specialized field such as sales, finance, marketing, human resources, or international operations. These company branches need their own data management departments, of course, and they also need executives to lead them.

What Is the Future Outlook for Data Architects?

According to the Bureau of Labor Statistics, job growth for database administrators, a field including data architects, is projected at 11 percent through 2026, which is faster than average for all occupations. Because computers touch most segments of life and work, there is a wealth of data that needs to be handled, organized, and stored. Somebody must set that information up in a way that is clear and user-friendly, and there is an expanding list of software languages and storage systems available to handle it. Entry is limited to those who can manage these complex tools, so the demand for data architects who can do the job should remain high.

Find Out More

CXL—Conversion Optimization Blog
website: https://conversionxl.com/blog
This blog by the CXL Institute offers a good overview of the data architecture field in the post "Getting the Website Information

Architecture Right: How to Structure Your Site for Optimal User Experiences." This blog post explores the best ways to organize information on a website, the most effective ways to deal with customers and their data, and how to handle metadata and define its uses.

DataScienceGraduatePrograms.com
website:www.datasciencegraduateprograms.com

This site's 2018 Data Science Scholarship Guide gathers all the current data science scholarship programs into one location. There are sections on qualifying for a data science scholarship, as well as a directory of all scholarships available at both the national and state levels, from business, government, and educational sponsors.

ICrunchData
website: https://icrunchdata.com

More than a job board, ICrunchData carries a wealth of news and information on data science, along with useful tips for jobseekers, who can post their résumés for companies that are looking for new talent. The site also publishes a regular newsletter to keep users up-to-date on the data science field.

KDnuggets
website: www.kdnuggets.com

A site covering data science and other tech fields, KDnuggets features blogs, newsletters, and lots of information on courses, bootcamps, seminars, and other learning events. This is also one of the leading job boards for data scientists and a great place to learn about companies that are hiring.

Roboticist

What Does a Roboticist Do?

Robots have long been used on assembly lines to make cars, computers, and other complicated machinery. Now they are becoming a fact of daily life for surgeons in operating rooms, miners in underground environments, and assemblers in factories of all kinds. A roboticist programs the machines using a pendant, which is a handheld box with a keypad and a joystick. The pendant controls the movement of the robotic arms, recording the movements, actions, and measurements in sequence for whatever the task needs. The roboticist also uses logic commands such as "go to," "wait," and "if" to teach the robot.

A good background in computer programming helps roboticists entering the profession. Mechanical aptitude helps as well—roboticists love to build things, and many of them started out creating bots or drones at home or in school. But industrial robots are much more complex than hobby gadgets. It can take years to master robot programming and get the machines to their optimum speed and efficiency. Complex operations require long instruction sets, hundreds of different logic functions, and constant repositioning in three dimensions.

That particular job is the reason why skilled roboticists need to learn several programming languages. Hardware description languages allow a roboticist to program field-programmable gate arrays, which are electronic circuits that can be configured in the field after they are manufactured.

Hands-on experience is the best preparation for a job in robotics. Many high schools and colleges offer robotics workshops where students work with robotic gear donated by local companies. In an interview on NASA's website, Julie Townsend, who works on the Mars Exploration Rover, explains how one such class was important to her. "I learned that the robot you design is not always the robot that works," Townsend says. "It was through these projects that I gained confidence in my own ability to learn whatever new skill was needed to complete the task at hand. If you don't know how to do something, that doesn't mean you can't do it—you just have to do some learning first."

As a roboticist's career progresses, he or she may specialize in one phase or another of the job. In the planning and prototype stages, roboticists build simpler, less expensive models to test the limits of what a machine can do. A prototype robot may be sent deep into a mineshaft, for example, to see if it can carry out a task consistently under dangerous conditions.

The jobs of roboticists are varied. Some specialize in programming control software. Others work as consultants, advising customers on the installation, use, and maintenance of the machines. Robotic engineers get into the nuts and bolts: motors, pistons, gears, wheels, sensors, robotic arms, and servomotors that must be designed, assembled, and configured to make up the physical machine.

Designers work on the cutting edge of the field, and often hold the most prestigious and well-paid jobs. A designer may be working on microscopic nanorobots, which can be injected into the bloodstream to fight bacteria or target cancer cells for destruction. Robots can also be designed to help disabled people. When asked on the site Hack the Union about the coolest project she ever worked on, roboticist M. Bernadine Dias answered, "I guess I'll pick my newest project—assistive robots for blind travelers. We are exploring how different types of robots can effectively interact with and assist blind people in the context of future urban travel."

The field of robotics is moving into new sectors of the economy, as the possible applications for machines multiply. Millions of jobs available today will be eliminated by robots. The manufacturing sector is going through a transformation—and that is not necessarily bad. "A lot of the people in manufacturing are men deep into their 50s, many about to retire," Jim Lawton of Rethink Robotics told an interviewer on the website *New Equipment Digest*. "Millennials don't want to do manufacturing jobs. Parents are not encouraging their kids to get into manufacturing. Finding qualified people is a struggle." Robots, however, can be programmed to do many of these tasks and fill the vital need in manufacturing industries.

Change is an inevitable fact of economic life, and companies in competitive businesses must work as efficiently as possible. That does not necessarily mean a net loss of jobs, however, because robots must be designed, built, programmed, operated, and maintained—all of which are tasks for their human creators.

How Do You Become a Roboticist?

Education

Most roboticists enter the field with a bachelor's degree. Good college majors for this career include mechanical, industrial, or electrical engineering; computer science; and even business administration—integrating robots into the supply chain and the manufacturing process is a key specialty in the robotics field.

Some entry-level tech jobs are open to those with associate's degrees. In the two-year electronics/robotics course at the Virginia Beach Technical School, students learn to integrate electronic, mechanical, hydraulic, and pneumatic systems and to build machines such as quadcopters and fully functional robots.

Many large universities now offer graduate degrees, even doctorates, in robotics engineering. One of the top programs is the Robotics Systems Development Program at Carnegie Mellon University in Pittsburgh, which combines tech skills with studies in business development and project management.

Certification and Licensing

Licensing of roboticists is not required, but some states require the licensing of professional engineers. Illinois, for example, requires that professional engineers who advertise their services register with the Department of Financial and Professional Regulation. They must have a bachelor's degree in engineering, possess four years of experience in the field (eight years if their degree is from a nonapproved engineering program), and pass an exam.

Certification can advance a career or get one started in this field. Some schools offer certification in the field of automation technology through classroom and online courses of study. These occupational certificates may include a specialty such as electrical engineering or artificial intelligence or demand courses in smart machine design, motor control, logic controllers, mapping, and programming.

Volunteer Work and Internships

A gig as a volunteer or intern with a robotics organization can help jump-start a career in automation technology. Volunteers are needed to run teaching programs, mentor engineering students at high schools, and host events such as robot competitions at which young people build and demonstrate their machines. Many companies have paid internship positions that give future roboticists a look at robotics development and programming. Dassault

Systèmes, a European three-dimensional software developer with an office in Auburn Hills, Michigan, offers twelve-week summer internships with the company's robotics development team. Interns assist in product design, simulations, and applications used for offline programming.

Skills and Personality

An engineering specialty such as robotics requires a strong interest in electrical and mechanical systems and an aptitude for assembling, maintaining, and repairing complex machinery. Roboticists must also be quick learners and have a sense of curiosity because the field is constantly changing. Strong math skills, problem-solving abilities, and knowledge of computer-aided design systems and software help, as do persistence and patience—a lot of trial and error is involved in building robotic prototypes and getting them ready for production.

On the Job

Employers

Roboticists often work for companies that design and manufacture robotic machines. But they are also employed by companies that use robots for highly repetitive or dangerous work, such as auto and textile manufacturers, mining companies, and computer makers. Amazon, a huge online retailer, needs to maintain fleets of mobile robots to work in its warehouses. The company hires many robotics engineers to program and maintain the machines. The Intelligent Robotics Laboratory, a division of aerospace company Lockheed Martin, needs engineers for artificial intelligence projects contracted by the US Department of Defense. These roboticists concentrate on intelligent autonomy, in which robots are programmed to perceive, plan, and reason as humans do.

Working Conditions

Roboticists work indoors, generally under conditions similar to those of the robots they build and program. During an install or servicing project, they may spend much of their time on assembly lines or factory floors or in warehouses or other industrial environments. Designing robots means working at a desk on computer-assisted design programs as well as drawing up specifications, cost estimates, quality control reports, and efficiency studies. Analyzing data is a major part of the job, but the assembling of prototypes and production robots takes place in labs or workrooms or on industrial production floors. These can be noisy, hazardous environments, and safety gear such as goggles and hardhats are required.

Roboticists normally work under project deadlines, meaning there can be some time pressure involved. They work in teams, and answer to supervisors or project leads who make sure the assigned tasks proceed on schedule. A roboticist working with a client may need to travel frequently and work on-site.

Earnings

Annual earnings for all types of electromechanical technicians (including roboticists) are from $36,550 to $87,970, according to the Bureau of Labor Statistics (BLS) . Earnings increase with education level, experience, and responsibility. Another factor is location. In cities such as New York; Washington, DC; and Los Angeles, where the cost of living is higher, a skilled roboticist can command a salary of $115,000 or more. In cities with a lower cost of living, such as Austin, Texas, or Salt Lake City, Utah, salaries average a bit less. The federal government pays the highest average salaries to robotics engineers and other skilled tech labor; the private sector runs a close second. State and local governments pay less, on average.

Opportunities for Advancement

There is a wide range of job descriptions in robotics. After starting out as a technician or assembler, roboticists can move into better-paid engineering jobs. With experience, those with the right management skills can become project leads, and skilled techs can move into chief engineer jobs. The next rung on the ladder includes supervisory and management jobs or an engineering specialization such as artificial intelligence or medical robots, where expertise is in demand and well paid. The educational field needs teachers, and colleges are setting up robotics departments with full professors who mentor future engineers. Roboticists who value their independence can become freelance contractors, lending their skills to companies on a temporary basis, or sales representatives who call on customers for robotics manufacturers.

What Is the Future Outlook for Roboticists?

According to the BLS, average job growth of 4 percent per year is expected for all electromechanical technicians. Creative roboticists envision their machines entering new sectors of the economy, such as food service and health care, and doing tasks with greater efficiency than that of human workers. That means an expanding field for workers who can adapt their skills to robotics engineering, design, maintenance, and operation—as well as the marketing and sales of robots and teaching of future roboticists in high schools, vocational schools, and colleges.

Find Out More

IEEE Robotics and Automation Society (RAS)
445 Hoes Ln.
Piscataway, NJ 08854
website: www.ieee-ras.org

This big, informative site from the Institute of Electrical and Electronics Engineers offers all the latest developments in the robotics fields. There are blog postings, full-length articles, and a schedule of RAS town halls, lectures, conferences, and other events around the globe. Users can also explore job offerings for robotics engineers.

International Federation of Robotics (IFR)
Lyoner Str. 18
60528 Frankfurt
Germany
website: https://ifr.org

The IFR is a trade group focused on changes in industry and the wider world by robotics. Its website presents a range of articles on lab research, company case studies, standardization, service robots, industrial robots, and the group's favorite theme: the creation of new jobs and careers through the roboticization of manufacturing.

NASA Robotics Alliance Project
website: https://robotics.nasa.gov

The project's website includes the "Educational Robotics Matrix," which is a table display of courses, competitions, events, and internships for all levels, from primary grades through graduate-level students. The matrix is laid out with simple titles and short descriptions, followed by a link taking the user to the appropriate website for more detail and contact information.

Robotics Online
website: www.robotics.org

This website offers many detailed, well-researched articles on automation breakthroughs and is a good place to learn about the future worlds made possible by robotics. Under the Robotic Resources tab, users will find a Beginner's Guide, Ask an Expert, and a Career Center listing jobs in engineering, management, manufacturing, marketing, and sales.

Game Developer

Game Developer

Minimum Educational Requirements
Bachelor's degree in computer science, software engineering, math, or information systems; associate's degree accepted for some entry-level jobs

Personal Qualities
Ability to work on a team; communication skills; high interest in game logic and gaming systems

Certification and Licensing
Licensing is not required; certification in relevant software languages may be helpful

Working Conditions
Indoors, working on desktop and laptop computers, often under pressure on a strict schedule for game release

Salary Range
From $54,000 to $127,000 annually

Number of Jobs
65,000 in 2015

Future Job Outlook
Projected job growth of 8 percent per year through 2026, which is average

What Does a Game Developer Do?

Game developer is a broad term for someone who imagines, designs, and writes code for a console or computer video game. Most game developers work as part of a development team, generating a game's images, gameplay, dialogue, and environments. There are many specialties in the field for each team member. A physics programmer, for example, writes code needed to simulate the properties of the physical world, such as light, sound, and gravity. Graphic designers give the game its look, and writers create its dialogue and text. Network specialists develop the capabilities needed to play the game online and with (or against) other players.

For a major studio, game developers work in teams that are responsible for various aspects of a years-long project. There are artists, programmers, designers, and audio developers, all working un-

32

der the supervision of producers. Game designers come up with the characters, roles, gameplay, and structure of the game, and programmers write the code to realize the design vision. In many cases, a lot of money is on the line; for top-of-the-line blockbuster games, prepared by major publishers, development budgets can run up to $30 million. Conversely, games designed for smartphones are much less elaborate and costly, and some have been created by smaller teams and even individuals.

Although creating a game can be fun, it is hard and often frustrating work. The pressure of meeting deadlines is one constant worry for developers, but there are many others. According to game developer David Mullich, who was interviewed on the Mashable website,

> Days are usually spent either in meetings or staring at a computer screen. The work can sometimes be monotonous, as you are often required to do simple but precise tasks over and over again. The stress level can be high as publishers make unrealistic demands in order to get maximum value for their investment, and the results are inevitably disappointing, for which the developer inevitably gets the blame.

There are several main genres in the game industry, each with its own unique development process. For a first-person shooter game, for example, the process begins with a story and continues with the development of characters and a setting. Developers then come up with weapons, abilities, and tools and graphic artists sketch out settings and environments. Game levels that become increasingly difficult as the game moves along are created; to move up, players have to solve new puzzles, deal with new enemies, and conquer other issues. Game developers are always balancing difficulty with playability.

Storyboards help the design team visualize the game. Whereas some are done on paper, others are rendered with animation and three-dimensional programs. Game programmers then write the code that computers and consoles read to render the game on the screen. A programmer uses one or more software languages and algorithms used to imitate real-world actions, such as the movement of a car or the flips and jumps of a skateboarder. Many game developers employ the frameworks used in previous games to avoid a lot of unnecessary and repetitive coding.

When a beta version of the game is done, testing begins. This is when developers must bring their skills, endurance, and patience. They must play through the game, over and over, to find and correct design flaws and programming bugs and try to improve the gameplay. One anonymous former game developer, interviewed on the *Guardian's* website, recalls that "at my studio you needed to have the 'passion' for a project to work six days a week, or put in 16-hour days. This is very much prevalent in the game industry and is seen as pulling out all the stops for your love of the project."

Aside from an insane work ethic, game developers need to have both technical and creative talent. They translate the vision of a game into programming languages, building tools such as level editors that can be used by other game designers. They know several important scripting languages, and they are constantly learning new languages to provide better tools and wider capabilities. Changing technology and platforms is exciting for developers because they have a passion for games. This enthusiasm carries developers through precarious times, when roles change and jobs disappear. The game industry is short on job security; games and systems go in and out of style, and companies—especially smaller independent shops—regularly close their doors. But good developers follow changes in the industry and the gaming community, hoping to stay in the market that they love.

How Do You Become a Game Developer?

Education
Entry-level jobs in this field require some higher education, with many game studios expecting a bachelor's degree with majors

in relevant subjects such as computer science, graphic arts, or software programming. Some schools offer degrees in game design and development, with courses in software engineering, computer science, and graphic design. If a future developer pursues some other college major, courses in animation, modeling, level design, interface design, drawing, creative writing, and storyboarding will introduce the specific skills needed by the industry. Membership in a game design club or on a gaming team also shows employers that an applicant is taking things seriously by keeping current with trends.

Certification and Licensing

There is no licensing requirement for game developers, but certification in software development from a major publisher, such as Microsoft, or in a relevant language, such as Java or C++, can boost an applicant's prospects. The Microsoft technology associate certification is aimed at high school and college students who want to show they have basic skills; it offers game development as a subspecialty. There are plenty of online courses and programs that will provide a certificate in game development at the end of a short course and after completion of an examination.

Volunteer Work and Internships

Most game producers want job applicants to have experience, and one of the best ways to gain experience is through an internship. Large companies offer internships to students looking for some hands-on experience in the gaming industry. At Nintendo, Ubisoft, and EA, there are technical and nontechnical internship positions, both paid and unpaid. Most take place in the spring or summer. Some of these big studios, such as Activision, require that interns complete freshman year in college. While working with a design team, an intern can pull together a portfolio, make contacts, and try out for a future employer.

Another good entry on a developer's résumé is volunteer work with a school course or summer camp for software coding or

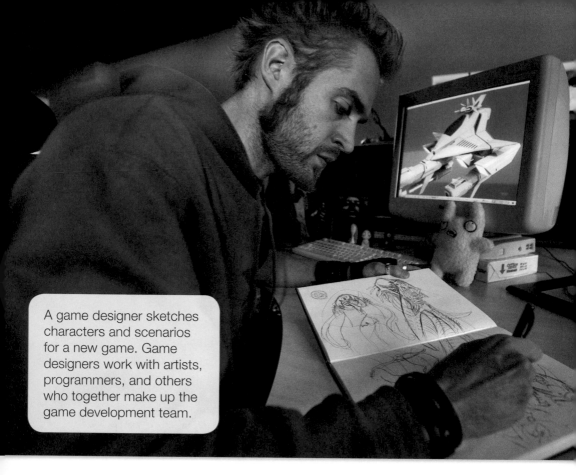

A game designer sketches characters and scenarios for a new game. Game designers work with artists, programmers, and others who together make up the game development team.

game design. Teaching is a great way to learn—it requires mastery of the subject, whether it is graphic design, software languages, or scriptwriting.

Skills and Personality

Game developers must be goal-oriented people who strive for perfection and obsess over details. A thick skin is also required: developers are under the constant scrutiny of peers and bosses who expect high-quality work. The job requires a combination of technical know-how and a creative sense. If working on art or environment, developers must be conscious of the capabilities of the software; if writing code, they must be sensitive to the game's appearance and style. Developers must be team players with good communication skills because all studio games rely on working with others who share the passion for putting out an excellent product. Other helpful traits are a love of math, logic skills, and patience.

On the Job

Employers

At one time, there were more than two thousand independent computer and video game studios at work in the United States. By 2018, the industry was consolidating. Too many games were unable to recoup their production costs, and big publishers brought game development in house rather than contracting to outside studios. There are a few major independent studios that own the big franchise games, which have become major ongoing, multimillion-dollar projects. There are also small studios that work as subcontractors, or independently, crafting just a few titles with a staff of a dozen or less. Game developers can also work as freelancing independents, working temporarily on assignments and moving from one project to the next.

Working Conditions

Game developers work indoors and spend much of their time on computers. Sometimes they attend meetings in which teams hash out their development strategy for games assigned to them. When a game is in active development and facing a release deadline, every team member's job can be stressful. There is intense competition in the field and pressure to come up with innovative gameplay and environments that will attract the dollars of fickle gaming consumers. Games can take years to reach their release date, and developers often face late nights, overtime, and—in many cases—the frustration of seeing their efforts go for nothing if the studio drops the game or it fails to reach a wide audience.

Earnings

Average annual base pay for game developers reached $85,877 in 2018. According to the Bureau of Labor Statistics, the range in this industry is wide, with novice developers earning around $54,000 a year and highly skilled, experienced developers making $127,000 or more. Key employees for public companies can earn stock options. Bonuses and profit sharing are nice features when a game company has a successful year. Salaries are higher at the bigger, more established studios, while smaller shops pay less in salary, with some offering only a share of game revenues as compensation.

Opportunities for Advancement

A game developer with experience can move up the ladder to lead designer or developer, with responsibility for the work of a team. Management positions in finance, accounting, business development, sales, and marketing will open to developers seeking to move out of the design studio into the higher corporate echelons. Those who enjoy high risks and high rewards move away from the company cubicles and build their own indie shops. "Being at the helm of a game company is exhilarating," reports Guillaume Boucher-Vidal on the game site Polygon. "It is also nerve wracking. The emotional roller coaster can be nearly unbearable at times. The pressure makes you feel like glass about to crack at any moment."

What Is the Future Outlook for Game Developers?

Gaming is growing. Traditional console games, making up about 80 percent of the game business, earned about $13 billion in 2015 and are projected to earn $16 billion in 2020. But in the entertainment world, games face competition from smart televisions; subscription services such as Netflix, Hulu, and Amazon Prime; and the crowded world of mobile apps. While smaller, independent studios struggle, major revenues are going to the big studios and franchise games. These titles earn much of their revenue through microtransactions, which are things like in-game purchases, expansion packs, premium content, and subscriptions. Game developers will thrive if they can adapt to industry changes and create innovative content for social media, gaming communities, and virtual reality.

Find Out More

Gamasutra

website: http://jobs.gamasutra.com

This website, devoted to game development jobs, allows users to search by job type, platform, and employer. A blog on the site keeps up-to-date on recent news in the major gaming sectors: consoles and computers, smartphones and tablets, independent, social and online, and virtual reality and augmented reality games.

GameDevMap

website: https://gamedevmap.com

GameDevMap, which calls itself a "living map and catalog of game development organizations," provides an interesting graphic database of the industry. The home page shows a world map with red dots indicating various locations where game companies are currently at work. Clicking on a dot shows local companies with more specific data and links to company websites.

GameJobHunter

website: https://gamejobhunter.com

A blog on this site keeps users up-to-date on recent happenings in the fickle gaming industry, with good news about start-ups and expansions as well as bad news about shutdowns, layoffs, and cutbacks.

GameRecruiter

website: www.gamerecruiter.com

This site has been around for twenty-five years, providing recruitment services to gaming employers as well as career counseling to developers. It includes a blog with career advice for new entrants to the field.

Mobile Developer

Mobile Developer

Minimum Educational Requirements
Bachelor's or associate's degree in software development or related computer science field

Personal Qualities
Aptitude for mathematics; talent for organization and communication; problem-solving abilities

Certification and Licensing
Licensing is not required; certification is available to help with career advancement

Working Conditions
Working at a desk on laptops or desktop systems; many mobile developers work as independent freelancers

Salary Range
From $70,000 to $135,000 annually

Number of Jobs
About 600,000, including employee and freelance positions

Future Job Outlook
Projected growth of 24 percent for all software developers through 2026, which is much faster than average

What Does a Mobile Developer Do?

A mobile developer creates apps for smartphone platforms such as Android and the iOS system used in Apple products. They use programming languages to write these apps. Each platform has a core language, and most app developers specialize in a certain platform. An Apple developer, for example, needs to know Objective-C and Swift, which are important languages used for iPhone apps. Android developers use Java, C++, C#, Kotlin, and several other languages.

Yet there is more to mobile development than just learning to code phone apps. A crucial part of the job is working with application programming interfaces (APIs). These serve as intermediaries between two programs, so that the information on one can easily be used by the other. For example, a new catering app may need to access Google's calendar feature to schedule events—a well-designed API makes that possible.

Another busy, in-demand sector for mobile developers is adapting websites to mobile platforms. There is a high demand for this service, as the public is devoting more of its time and attention to smartphones. A web page that cannot load on a phone's smaller screen is almost useless for big clients, so mobile techs repurpose the website's settings and design. They often have to cut text and images and create buttons, links, and fillable forms to make the site useful.

Although mobile developers need to be creative, they do not spend a lot of time dreaming up new apps. Testing, maintaining, and routinely updating apps demand a lot of a developer's day. A big part of the process is debugging code that has one glitch or another that slows or stops the app. Another consideration is efficiency—if the app requires too much speed or memory, it will need to be streamlined.

Mobile developers also must consider user experience, meaning how a user interacts with the app. A user-friendly site is the goal of all mobile developers, no matter what platform they are using. In an online interview for software development shop Glance, London-based Ron Novak of Segue Technologies comments that "one of the most important trends in IT [information technology] is the expectation that the user experience will be similar on or customized for, all screens and device sizes." Developers must ensure that app versions of websites are concise yet functional for small screens so that users feel comfortable on the platform.

Most mobile developers do not work alone. This job often requires teamwork to see an app to completion. The job also requires contact with clients to ensure their needs are met when building apps. A ride-sharing company such as Uber, for example, needs phone-based data systems that allow customers to order trips and drivers to find their riders and get directions. Another client, such as the Weather Channel, may want to make its weather data and radar imagery available to the public on smartphones. Mobile developers turn these requests into usable apps.

A good mobile developer also has to keep up with the constant changes in the industry. New programming languages are always coming into use, and platforms are constantly being revised and updated. Every time a new Samsung Galaxy or Apple iPhone comes out, a new generation of apps, or at least app updates, is needed. Cameron Hotchkies of ATX Innovation explains how difficult it is to build apps for operating systems that are always evolving or are customized for specific phone manufacturers. In an interview on the company's website, he states, "With Android, you have . . . nine or ten different versions sitting in the marketplace. And then on top of that you might have version 2.2 but you'd have Motorola's own different version of 2.2 . . . and with all the extra junk that they stick into the operating system, you basically have to go out and pick up as many different devices as you can." But this kind of work keeps a lot of people busy—globally, there will be 14 million mobile developers by 2020, more than half of all software developers in the world.

The best mobile developers command big salaries and have no lack of rewarding work available to them. Interviewed by the website CNN Money, developer Kyle Craig comments, "Mobile app developers are the first to test out the latest phones, tablets and wearable devices. If you like playing around with technology and exploring all the possibilities it offers, this can be a really fun job."

How Do You Become a Mobile Developer?

Education

Mobile developers prepare for their careers with degrees in computer science, software development, engineering, or other tech-related fields. Top app development courses are hosted by the Massachusetts Institute of Technology; Carnegie Mellon University; the University of California, Berkeley; and New York University. Employers may require a bachelor's degree as a minimum, but a certificate course at a vocational-technical school or an associate's degree from a junior college may also suffice for an entry-level position.

There are plenty of online courses in app development, which can be useful for showing some knowledge and experience with mobile technology. The source of the course is key—employers prefer certificates from traditional, top-ranked universities over education companies specializing, or limited to, virtual classrooms.

Stanford University, for example, one of the nation's top technology centers, offers the Developing Apps for the iPhone and iPad online course. This free course is sponsored by Apple and relies heavily on the company's current consumer products. No beginners are allowed—the course requires knowledge of programming, and it recommends knowledge of UNIX systems, graphics, and databases.

Certification and Licensing

No license is required to work as a mobile developer, but certification, especially from a major company such as Microsoft, Apple, or Google, will show a potential employer expertise and a specialization that can help an applicant land a better-paying job. The Microsoft technology associate certifications, for example, are an excellent way for advanced students to get some direct industry experience—and they never expire. These certifications start with the software development fundamentals credential, which paves the way for more advanced certifications, such as the Microsoft certified solutions developer.

Other relevant professional certifications include the Kony certified developer, which is tied to a big mobile application development platform provider. IBM offers the certified mobile application developer, and Google offers the associate Android developer designation. These certifications often require some previous experience with software languages or relevant work experience, and all impose a tough examination in order to complete the course.

Volunteer Work and Internships

Mobile app developers have many opportunities for rewarding volunteer work, including creating apps for charitable organizations such as the Red Cross, the American Lung Association, and Doctors Without Borders. The Peace Corps, which operates in foreign lands to help with education, public health, and housing, creates apps that translate local languages and dialects. Instead of searching out posted positions and competing with other applicants, creative and energetic developers can study a need, dream up their own app, and reach out with the idea to a potential client.

Internships provide a path to employment at many companies. Applicants can be selective because the field is growing fast and the demand for their contribution is high. A recent search on the employment website Indeed turned up internships at Savvy Technology Solutions, Reach Mobi, Menlo Technologies, and dozens of other small and midsize developers. Larger outfits, such as Google, Microsoft, and Apple, have big, organized internship programs that bring students into direct contact with the biggest players in the industry.

Skills and Personality

Mobile developers need a good knowledge of software languages such as C#, C++, Objective-C, and Java. They need to be organized and eager to learn, as it is easy to fall behind on the constant new generations of phones and devices. Math aptitude helps, as do communication and problem-solving skills. Mobile development is also a field in which a strong interest in culture, media, and consumer trends will help. Most apps must adjust to ever-changing public interests and trends, so keeping current not only on the technology but also the whims of the marketplace is essential.

On the Job

Employers

Most mobile developers work for big companies that produce apps for shopping, banking, travel, health care, and other services. These employers require the services of many skilled, dedicated techies to consistently build and provide upkeep for mobile applications. Media organizations such as Netflix and Disney are working at the edge of evolving technology as streaming services compete with traditional cable and movie theaters. Gaming companies also hire for mobile

Often working in teams, mobile developers create apps for smartphone platforms. Part of their job is to debug glitches that affect the smooth operation of the apps.

development; as franchises move from the console to handhelds to smartphones, each platform has a different set of capacities and design parameters. Almost every large company doing business in the twenty-first century is compelled to reach as many customers as possible across as many platforms as possible. Therefore, mobile developers will likely be in demand for the foreseeable future.

Working Conditions

Writing code for mobile applications is a desk job that can involve long hours of keyboarding. The job also entails making phone calls, attending meetings, and, for independents, engaging in some travel to meet with a development team or clients. Employers may have big staffs or small departments, or they may hire freelancers for temporary assignments. Freelancers do not need much more than a good Internet connection, a software development kit, and a place for their desktop or laptop computers to function efficiently.

Earnings

Mobile developers command some of the highest average salaries in the tech world. According to the Bureau of Labor Statistics, the average annual wage reached $103,202 in 2018, with a range of $70,000 to $135,000. Salaries are generally higher at companies such as Facebook, Yahoo!, and eBay, which rely on apps to do business. Financial, health care, and retail companies pay more average salaries, and public employers such as school districts typically pay a bit less.

Opportunities for Advancement

With experience, a mobile developer can move into leadership ranks as a team leader or department manager. Developer jobs can also open the door to executive tech positions, such as chief information officer. Although independents may not have opportunities for advancement, making and keeping contacts in the industry can assure a steady stream of work.

What Is the Future Outlook for Mobile Developers?

By 2018 the worldwide market for mobile phones was expanding rapidly, with more than 5 billion subscribers. For many people, these devices have become an essential part of their day, which means the demand is also on the rise for new, interesting ways to use them. Many development companies are focusing solely on mobile development, meaning they are leaving the web and personal computer work to dedicate themselves to mobile platforms. It adds up to a hot and flexible market for skilled mobile developers, who are well-known for jumping from one employer to the next in constant search of a position that best suits their skills and interests.

Find Out More

Amazon Web Services (AWS)
website: https://aws.amazon.com

The AWS website includes a page titled "What Is Mobile Application Development?," which provides an excellent introduction to the process of building mobile apps. There are sections on app life cycles, back-end and front-end services, the different platforms, and native versus hybrid applications. Links to the AWS Mobile Hub give users an opportunity to build their own apps with step-by-step guidance.

ITCareerFinder
website: www.itcareerfinder.com

This website is dedicated to careers in information technology. Its web page entitled "Mobile Application Developer" provides a solid introduction to the job of mobile developer. It lists all major platforms, core languages, and development environments. There are also links to courses; certification and degree programs; and straightforward descriptions of jobs, the skills and responsibilities required, average salaries, and education requirements.

My Life with Android
website: http://mylifewithandroid.blogspot.com

This is a blog about creating apps for Android phones. Author Gabor Pellar goes into detail about his working process and the many smart inventions he has created using Android operating systems. Schematics, pictures, code, and other information is presented in plain language, giving even beginners insight into the life and work of a mobile app developer.

Pluralsight
website: www.pluralsight.com

This is a well-designed and very usable technology learning site that keeps visitors up on the news and training in mobile software and apps. There are dozens of courses (with free trials offered) in subjects such as C# programming, Google Android development, and Microsoft Azure services, as well as webinars, blogs, and a guide to becoming a developer.

User Experience Designer

User Experience Designer

Minimum Educational Requirements
Associate's degree in a field related to computer science, software engineering, or visual design

Personal Qualities
Time management, problem-solving, and communication skills; strong visual design sense; creativity

Certification and Licensing
Licensing is not required; certification is available and may help with career advancement

Working Conditions
Indoors, working on desktops and laptops, either independently or on location with an employer; client meetings and travel are sometimes required

Salary Range
From $69,000 to $120,000 annually

Number of Jobs
About 238,000 employed as either user experience or user interface designers

Future Job Outlook
Projected growth of 10 percent through 2028, which is faster than average

What Does a User Experience Designer Do?

Websites and mobile apps can be fun, entertaining, and useful—or slow, clunky, and frustrating. The problem of making software a good experience falls to the user experience (UX) designer, also known as the user interface (UI) designer. UX is a relatively new field in tech, but it is a fast-growing and well-paid job, and the skills it demands are needed by software companies, computer makers, and mobile app providers.

It is easy to understand the growing need for UX designers. A web presence is required for retailers, service providers, libraries, government agencies—anyone who runs a business or organization in the digital age. To grab their customers' attention and make it easy for them to interact with the site or application, that web presence must be user-friendly. If a business application, for example, is hard to use, confusing, or slow, then customers will go to competitors to buy the stuff they want. UX designers strive to make sure such problems do not happen and that customers or visitors are met with satisfying, user-friendly interfaces.

To do their work, UX designers draw on research. They read surveys, study workflow analysis, examine website or mobile app data on page visits and click-throughs, and test their work through beta versions. On her blog for the Adobe company, French UX designer Sandrine Tizaoui reports that simply browsing online is a very necessary part of her work. "I spend most of my early afternoons browsing on Twitter, Medium, and other platforms and favourite blogs on the hunt for interesting ideas and articles to read. If something grabs my attention, I take notes, so I can come back to it later in the day. I also spend a lot of time checking other UX/UI designers' works for inspiration, especially the use cases." Finding out what users want and why they have not found the perfect application helps Tizaoui and others address these challenges in the apps on which they work.

The job demands a creative, right-brain capacity, a sense for how a certain client's website, or mobile app, should look and feel. Selling skateboards online, for example, demands a very different UX approach than providing bank account information or designing an interactive museum page. For any client, branding—how to present one's self to the public—is crucial.

UX techs also need intuition for how people will react to the instructions, images, and text on a page, and that means keen insight into human psychology. "One of my favorite things to do," UX designer Yael Levy writes on her blog "I Am Not My Pixels,"

> is the stage where I get to talk to people about their world.
> . . . Other times, I get to watch people actually use something I've designed. I'm able to see how people actually use

49

the web and technology and bear witness to the myriads of different ways that this happens. I love getting this peek into people's minds, digging a little and coming back with nuggets of information about what makes them tick.

UX designers build the navigation tools a customer uses to get from one screen or page to the next. They create the detail pages that present products to the public and place the text and images where this presentation will be clear and effective. They test usability, speed, loading times, and public feedback, and they report on these metrics to clients and management.

A UX designer may spend a lot of time in meetings or on the phone, consulting with customers and learning their goals. For someone working independently, this client communication means a lot of phone work and travel as well as adapting to the very different demands and styles of different clients. "Currently one of my clients is a 2-hour train-ride away, one is a 10-minute bike ride away, and other clients I work with from home," reports independent UX designer Matthew Magain on the UXMastery website. "Some have plenty of budget for extensive user research, others can barely be convinced to include one round of user testing before launch." Magain's comment shows that clients have different demands and limitations, and a UX designer must work with each one to provide the best results.

To create sites, UX designers need to build storyboards, site maps, and wireframes—skeletal graphic outlines of a website that show how it will flow from one page and function to the next. A requirement for this job is a good knowledge of graphic design and software such as Photoshop, Illustrator, and Fireworks. UX designers should know how to edit photos, use Cascading Style Sheets (CSS), and design a web page. They also work with software developers and engineers, who provide the storage and processing power that make a website function.

A lot of collaboration is involved, even if a UX tech works independently, moving from one project to the next for different clients and companies. That demands the ability to clearly communicate ideas and organize one's time and resources. Employers hiring UX designers look carefully for these so-called soft skills along with the hard knowledge of systems, software, and the technology behind the Internet and the wide world of smartphones and other handheld devices.

How Do You Become a User Experience Designer?

Education

Several educational pathways prepare students for a career as a UX designer. Relevant college degrees or majors include graphic design, computer science, software development, communications, and psychology. UX design courses are offered at the undergraduate level, and Associate's degrees are available in software or mobile development that will get the attention of a potential employer.

At the graduate level, more specialized degree courses are usually available for students who already have a bachelor's degree in a tech field. Southern New Hampshire University, for example, offers a master's in information technology with concentrations in database design or web design, and the graduate education programs at the University of Minnesota and Purdue University list a learning design and technology concentration that can broaden the skillset of a UX designer.

Certification and Licensing

No license is required in this field, but certification programs abound that offer students and professionals advanced, specialized knowledge in UX design. The Nielsen Norman Group, Human Factors International, and San Francisco State University all offer UX certification programs, and the Weinschenk Institute has a series of UX courses—some of them free—that focus on human online behavior. Many certification courses in the field can be completed in a reasonably short amount of time and can boost a job applicant's knowledge and preparation.

Volunteer Work and Internships

UX design volunteers are in demand to assist nonprofits and charities, many of which have limited budgets for their apps and web pages. The website VolunteerMatch, which pairs tech volunteers with these organizations, lists numerous opportunities to help out and gain experience. Volunteers can also visit the Red Cross, the American Lung Association, and other nonprofits directly to inquire about volunteer opportunities.

Many large companies use internships as a recruiting tool, developing new full-time staff through the process. A useful route to finding an internship is to go directly to a company website and search for a careers page or search job sites for openings. Internships.com is a site focused on both unpaid and paid temporary positions for students and novices, and it routinely lists UX design positions.

Skills and Personality

A familiarity with certain programming languages, including Java, Perl, and CSS, is expected of UX designers. Hypertext markup language, or HTML, is the code used to design on the World Wide Web, and it is essential for anyone working on the design and functions of a web page. Other useful skills include a good working knowledge of Photoshop, Dreamweaver, and Illustrator. UX designers need a creative streak, an interest in the development of web pages and mobile apps, and an aptitude for graphic and visual design. There is a problem-solving element as well. Making pages and apps function properly can take UX designers along a difficult road of software bugs, processor slowdowns, coding errors, and system issues, so patience is also an important trait.

Employers

Big tech companies such as Microsoft, Apple, Google, and IBM hire large staffs of UX designers to create their public web pages and mobile apps. Retailers, public universities, government agencies, health care professionals, and hospitals also need user-friendly design but might not retain dedicated designers. Indeed, most people in this field work freelance, moving from one client to the next either on their own or through an agency that markets their talents.

Working Conditions

UX is an indoor desk job, but it also might involve some travel to meet clients and prospective customers or to attend conferences. UX designers also engage their clients via telephone or on-site meetings, with many encounters now taking place over FaceTime and Skype. Time is spent studying new systems and software and, of course, keyboarding and working in front of a monitor. For those designers who work for a single employer, office time will include collaborating with a team.

Earnings

The job search website Glassdoor estimates the annual salary range for professional UX designers at $69,000 to $120,000. When offering salaries, employers take experience and skill level into account. For example, an applicant who specializes in designing UIs, one of the most important aspects of this job, would tend to draw a higher salary. Education level may also count, as does job location.

Opportunities for Advancement

UX designers can advance into better-paid specialties. With some years of experience, UX designers can move into desktop software or mobile app design and apply their knowledge to creating new programs. They also might move into a management position, leading a team on major projects, or strike out on their own as a freelance UX consultant, with no limit on earnings. Those with UX knowledge also might find positions in education because many colleges are seeing increasing enrollments in computer science and software design courses.

What Is the Future Outlook for User Experience Designers?

In sectors such as retail clothing, restaurants, automotive, and entertainment media, the competition for customers has always been fierce, and now websites and mobile apps are a vital part of marketing products or advertising services. The easier the screens and buttons on these apps are to use, the better the chance for a satisfied and loyal customer. That means UX design is a high-demand skill throughout the economy, and the profession will flourish both for freelancers and employees in the years to come. As websites migrate to mobile devices, the knowledge of how to make these smaller screens as user-friendly as possible will become one of the most needed specialties in the tech universe.

Find Out More

User Experience Professionals Association
website: http://uxpa.org

This organization's useful site maintains portals to blogs, books, white papers, journals, career consulting services, and a calendar of its many conferences, workshops, and education offerings. The "Job Bank" section is open to nonmembers and is an excellent place to learn about the kinds of companies hiring and the UX-related positions they are creating.

UXBeginner

website: www.uxbeginner.com

A site designed for those just getting started as a UX design professional, UXBeginner offers an introduction to education, career choices, and portfolios. There are blog posts on "How to Find a UX Mentor," "Complete Guide to UX Resumes," and other interesting topics for anyone seeking a career in the field. The site's author also offers paid courses and career coaching.

UXMastery

PO Box 7101
Reservoir, VIC 3073
Australia
website: https://uxmastery.com

This site lists UX degree programs in the United States and around the world, with links to the web pages created by each program for further information, applications, and contact information. UXMastery also provides articles, resources, books, templates, courses, games, and a podcast.

UXPlanet

website: https://uxplanet.org

This site offers dozens of articles from a wide variety of authors on the concepts and best practices in UX design. One of its specialties is the subject of human/computer interaction and why some sites seem to easily attract and hold users and others never will. The UX career section offers advice to beginners and veterans on how to advance in the field.

Artificial Intelligence Specialist

At a Glance

Artificial Intelligence Specialist

Minimum Educational Requirements
Bachelor's degree with a major in computer science, engineering, math, software development, or statistics

Personal Qualities
Strong logical reasoning, problem-solving, mathematical, and communication skills; an affinity for teamwork

Certification and Licensing
Licensing is not required; professional certification programs are available

Working Conditions
Indoors, using desktop and laptop computers; sometimes in factories, robotics labs, and research centers

Salary Range
From $47,000 to $133,000 annually

Number of Jobs
About 27,900 for computer and information research scientists, which includes artificial intelligence specialists, in 2016

Future Job Outlook
Projected growth of 19 percent for all computer research and information scientists through 2026, which is faster than average

What Does an Artificial Intelligence Specialist Do?

The job of an artificial intelligence (AI) specialist is to make systems smarter—meaning more responsive to their environment, to incoming data, and to the needs of human operators. With AI software, for example, a doorbell becomes a security system, with cameras, voice or fingerprint recognition, and a live feed to a smartphone or desktop.

AI allows video games to respond, and change, according to a human gamer's unique style of play. It also permits smartphones and even robots to respond to voice commands; AI-built androids now provide the entire staff—reception, maintenance, window cleaners, and porters—at the Henn na Hotel in Sasebo, Japan. This is called applied AI, which takes the science and makes it practical for computer systems to recognize voices, interpret information, solve problems, speak, and react.

One of the most prominent AI technologies is the autonomous vehicle (AV). AVs now being road-tested can respond to any instructions from passengers and use an updated GPS database to navigate to the fastest routes.

There is a worldwide shortage of AI specialists, meaning demand is high, and the real experts in the field are paid insane salaries. But there is a catch: AI specialists must have a mastery of data systems, math, and programming, combined with a creative vision. In an interview on the website 80,000Hours, Jan Leike, an AI specialist at the British company DeepMind, suggests that AI specialists be prepared for working at the edge of the unknown. Leike states, "You should be comfortable with navigating a space that you don't really understand very well, because researchers kind of necessarily are on the frontier of human knowledge and things that we understand, so you have to be comfortable with the unknown."

The central idea of AI is to make computers and digital systems "think" like a human. Researchers in the field study how people make decisions and respond to new information. They look at logical reasoning, such as how a chess player works through many different possible moves to come up with an effective attack. They analyze the ability of the brain to understand language, to navigate to a location, or to solve a math problem. They also study memory and how people use it to guide their actions.

The key step in this process is to write algorithms that instruct machines on how to respond to incoming data. Yet it can be a mysterious process. AI specialists go through a lot of trial and error in their work, and they do not always understand why one method works but another does not. "There's an anguish in the field," Ali Rahimi, a Google researcher, tells *Science* magazine. "Many of us feel like we're operating on an alien technology."

The title *AI specialist* covers many different job roles and titles. Software engineers help build operating systems, applications, databases, and networks. They know all about software used to control devices, and they understand common coding languages. They apply this knowledge to processes such as traffic control, weather prediction, and speech recognition. Software engineers working in AI, for example, build digital assistants, such as Siri or Cortana, that respond to voiced questions. They are also installing systems in new cars that predict where drivers want to go based on their past behavior.

Another important job title in AI is *data scientist*. The job is to collect data—sometimes a lot of it—to test models of behavior and write algorithms that control the decisions a system makes. A background in math, statistics, or data management is crucial in the data science field, as is knowledge of how databases are put together. Much of the job involves keeping data "clean," which means it is free of mistakes or errors that render a data set useless for applying to models. Another specialty is predictive analysis, which decides the probability of one action in response to another. A smart home system, for example, might take in a weather report and send an order to a grocery delivery service in preparation for a coming blizzard.

Other AI professionals work as engineers, building industrial robots that carry out tasks once assigned to humans. With the use of AI software, a factory robot can slow production when inventory levels get too high or stop production when a batch is complete. An important branch of AI engineering is computer vision, which involves teaching systems to respond to visual data such as brightness, color, and shape. This is a vital part of AV technology, in which visual data must be interpreted and acted on by a mechanical system, often at high speeds and under hazardous road conditions.

The AI field is expanding the number of job descriptions listed under the official Bureau of Labor Statistics category of computer research and information scientist. As the technology develops and moves into new applications, AI will become a job sector on its own, with all those working in the field having the common task of making machines and data systems as smart and useful as possible.

How Do You Become an Artificial Intelligence Specialist?

Education

To get started in the AI field, applicants need a bachelor's degree in computer science, artificial intelligence, software development, systems engineering, or robotics. Courses in math, statistics, and logic provide good preparation for the work involving databases and datasets, and some knowledge of psychology helps in the effort to develop the "thinking" ability of systems and machines. Management or other leadership roles may demand a master's degree, and college-level teaching may require a doctorate.

Certification and Licensing

AI research requires no licensing, but certifications that show knowledge and experience in this field are available. A certificate of completion simply means a user has gone through an online course, such as the AI: Implications for Business Strategy course offered by the Massachusetts Institute of Technology's Sloan School of Management. Such certifications can help applicants land better jobs.

Volunteer Work and Internships

Volunteerism has taken hold in the AI field. Nonprofit organizations in many different sectors are employing AI technology to carry out their missions. A group devoted to sustainable farming, for example, can deploy predictive analysis to offer farmers information on when to plant and when to harvest. Charitable groups in health care, such as Doctors Without Borders, can use AI data and machine learning to predict disease outbreaks. It is also possible to volunteer for charities as a fund-raiser or social media liaison at conferences and workshops where the latest AI innovations are presented.

Research internships are plentiful in the AI field, whether at an AI think tank or a global corporation. SRI International, the Allen Institute for Artificial Intelligence, Forge.AI, Intel, VMware, and Baidu USA hire interns for machine-learning projects. Some of these are administrative jobs—desk jobs to help researchers hold to schedules and plan their work. Others allow interns to help with data management and programming.

Skills and Personality

To deal with this new frontier in technology, AI specialists need patience, persistence, and curiosity. They do not work alone, so an affinity for teamwork and shared goals is also important. They should know languages such as Python, C++, and Java, which are common tools in AI work. They also must be familiar with parallel processing and graphics processing unit programming. These technologies help AI programmers render complex data in a graphical format and apply the algorithms that teach machines to "think," to recognize patterns, and to make decisions. AI specialists need an excellent grasp of math and logic and must know how to construct models, set variables, and predict outcomes using software and computer systems.

On the Job

Employers

In the private sector, robotics companies are perhaps the most popular for job applicants with AI experience and certification, but many industries utilize robotics and AI programming as well. Automotive companies, electronics manufacturers, defense industries, computer makers, and communications firms are either using AI research or are interested in building new AI departments. The academic field also hires researchers and instructors in the field—many larger colleges and universities are setting up AI departments and research labs to experiment in the field and to train those who will shape it.

Working Conditions

The environment for AI specialists varies from desktop number crunching to factory-floor implementations. The field is new, so there is a hands-on quality to AI work, as machines are trained for their work and humans are trained to handle them. AI professionals do a lot of independent reading and research online and cooperate with teams to handle big projects. They may work long hours, and at any hour, since ideas can hit at any time without warning. AI research requires analytical thinking and problem-solving abilities that often function best when away from daily routines and a fixed workplace.

Earnings

Talented AI workers are in short supply, so salaries are among the highest in the tech field. According to Paysa, a site that studies job earnings, salaries for AI specialists range from $47,000 to $133,000. Larger tech companies pay specialists up to $500,000 annually, and they also offer signing bonuses and stock options. Most nonprofit organizations cannot match that kind of money unless they are well funded. One example is OpenAI, a nonprofit founded by Elon Musk and other tech bigwigs, which recruited notable machine-learning scientist Ilya Sutskever from Google for a salary of $1.9 million a year. "I turned down offers for multiple times the dollar amount I accepted at OpenAI," Sutskever told a *New York Times* interviewer. For specialists like Sutskever, the attraction of the work and its uses outweigh the lower pay.

Opportunities for Advancement

In the AI field, there are opportunities to advance to job titles such as lead researcher, department head, or project manager.

Education is one of the keys to promotion and advancement; many AI jobs specifically call for advanced degrees or doctorates as well as a demonstrated ability to initiate and complete a project with a real-world application. Seeking independence to pursue dream projects, many AI specialists form their own nonprofit institutions, research groups, or development companies to build and program machines.

What Is the Future Outlook for Artificial Intelligence Specialists?

Although the concept of artificial intelligence is about as old as computers, the AI field has been growing rapidly in the twenty-first century. Nor will there be any slowing down of new job opportunities and descriptions. As the field continues to advance with new concepts and applications, there will be a demand for AI specialists who understand these concepts and can present them to a world just beginning to adapt to smart machines.

Find Out More

Association for the Advancement of Artificial Intelligence (AAAI)
2275 E. Bayshore Rd., Suite 160
Palo Alto, CA 94303
website: www.aaai.org

This nonprofit society is devoted to studying the embodiment of human thought and intelligent behavior in machines. Through conferences and workshops, the AAAI promotes research in the AI field, encourages public understanding of AI, and keeps members current on new developments in the field.

IBMWatson

website: www.ibm.com/watson

IBM remains a dominant company in the tech field, and its Watson project, originally created to compete on the television game show *Jeopardy!*, is now a leader in natural language processing and AI research. The Watson site features webinars, case studies, and software development kits.

Intel AI Academy for Students

website: https://software.intel.com/ai-academy/students

This site features an introduction to the AI field for beginners, with hands-on learning courses for developers; articles on hot AI topics, such as blockchain and cryptocurrencies; a social network; and a student group. The site links students in the field, or the simply curious, to a corporation active in creating new AI applications for the commercial market.

Leap

website: https://leap.ai

This website advertises itself as an "intelligent digital career companion," applying AI to the field of employee recruiting. With just a few questions, the site aspires to match jobseekers to ideal employers, and employers to the best candidates. It is an interesting place to learn about the use of AI concepts and tools.

Website Developer

Website Developer

Minimum Educational Requirements
None; however, many employers require at least a high school diploma, with courses in computer science, marketing, or web design and development

Personal Qualities
Interest in coding, graphic design, and digital media; good communication and problem-solving skills

Certification and Licensing
No license is required; a wide variety of certifications are available from public and private organizations

Working Conditions
Indoors, on desktop and laptop computers; frequent meetings and phone contact with clients

Salary Range
From $36,000 to $122,000 annually

Number of Jobs
About 163,000 employees and freelancers as of 2016

Future Job Outlook
Predicted growth of 15 percent through 2026, which is faster than average

What Does a Website Developer Do?

The World Wide Web is a big place, and for skilled website developers, there is a lot of work to do. According to different estimates, there were 1.3 to 1.8 billion websites up and running as of 2018. Each of them must be created, designed, filled with content, and maintained. These are the basic tasks of website developers.

At one time, website developers built sites through a lot of monotonous coding in hypertext markup language (HTML) and other web-oriented programming languages. Many website developers assigned to functions such as e-mail and credit card transactions still do just that. "In order to complete these site-specific integrations, I extensively familiarize myself with the client's website, so as to write the code that jives perfectly with their existing code," explains Bethanne Zink, a developer interviewed on the code training website Skillcrush. "Today I'm writing code that hooks into the API [application programming interface] for the e-mail service provider of one of our e-commerce sites. It's a project that I've tackled for many of our other clients."

Some website developers have full-time office jobs, working for employers who need to keep their big websites fresh and responsive to the public. The majority, however, work independently to find their own clients, who hire them on a project-by-project basis to either create or upgrade their sites. These clients have a budget and scope—a range of capabilities they want their web pages to have—and they need designers who can manage their time efficiently.

The technical knowledge and skill needed by website developers does not mean it is a difficult field to enter, at least compared to many other tech jobs. But a website developer needs to have hands-on experience and build a portfolio of completed projects to acquire paying clients. When searching for full-time website developers, employers want some skills, including knowledge of object-oriented programming, HTML coding, user interface design, and how to build wireframe prototypes—the blueprints of websites. Developers must also use and understand social media and be able to read the essential metrics of site speed and traffic.

Furthermore, developers need mastery of a graphics program such as Photoshop, Illustrator, or Fireworks. They will have to mount animation, video, and audio on web pages, and they must be ready to use version-control systems such as Git, which keep track of a project as multiple users create, change, and maintain it. These are industrial-strength systems and programs, and even experienced developers are constantly learning how to use them. "I may be in Photoshop to whip up some graphics," explains Jeff Pollard on the website of Moz, an Internet marketing company. "If I'm ever making major changes to a design or page, I'll take a screenshot of the existing site, wipe the area I'm changing clean, and design the new component in Photoshop before I even start writing HTML. . . . Occasionally I'll be in IRC (Internet relay chat) asking questions or helping other users, just to keep knowledgeable on the technology I'm using."

Searching for answers and knowledge is also important. "You have to be proactive in troubleshooting and problem-solving independently, using the incredible plethora of knowledge and experiences documented across the interwebs," reports Rosie Allabarton on CareerFoundry, a mentoring site for web development. "When learning to become a web developer, Google will become your best friend."

Website developers also keep up on changes in web tech, such as the capabilities of major browsers such as Chrome and Firefox, and the state of search algorithms used by Google. Search engine optimization (SEO) is a very necessary skill; when competing for attention against more than a billion other sites, SEO is the way to get enough visitors to land on a page to make the time, effort, and expense worthwhile for a client.

Soft skills are also necessary in this profession. Website developers rarely work alone, so they need a strong teamwork mentality. They also must be persistent and patient since debugging and troubleshooting are a big part of the job. Problem-solving skills, attention to detail, and an ability to take suggestions, criticism, and less-than-supportive feedback are also essential. Website developers work in a very competitive, fast-changing field, and adapting themselves to the demands and needs of others will help them thrive.

How Do You Become a Website Developer?

Education

Designing websites requires a background in desktop publishing and some knowledge of key languages used to program web pages. Some designers teach themselves these skills, but most employers want to see a high school diploma with a good knowledge of computer science and graphic design. Training in multimedia tools such as Flash is also useful to make websites more engaging. For positions as webmaster or web administrator, more advanced tech skills are needed, and employers may require a two- or four-year degree as well as certification in web development, server administration, programming, or computer networking.

Certification and Licensing

Certification in the software and other tools used in web design and development will give job applicants an advantage. Large companies, who are in constant need of new web tech talent, offer their own certification programs. In 2018 the huge online retailer Amazon, for example, offered ten different certification programs, including certified developer, certified solutions architect, and certified cloud practitioner, the last being a course and exam in web-based cloud storage. Google and Microsoft also offer a long series of web-focused certification courses, and Adobe covers a range of web skills in its Adobe certified expert program. To complete these certifications, a passing grade on an examination is required; however, the sponsors offer online exam guides, preparation tips, and practice questions to smooth the way.

Volunteer Work and Internships

Nonprofit foundations and charities have websites too. They need designers to create their pages, and developers and administrators to maintain them. Many will accept volunteers who have some experience to offer and who are seeking credits for their résumés and page designs for their portfolios. The website VolunteerMatch provides hundreds of opportunities, sorted by "cause areas" (education, hunger, etc.), responsibilities, date posted, and location, with many available as work-from-home positions. The website Idealist lists thousands of volunteer and internship positions at nonprofits all over the world.

Internships for website developers are plentiful. A summer break gives students in the last year or two of their college careers an excellent chance to audition possible employers and vice versa. Skilled applicants can be selective; there are hundreds of internships offered by companies large and small, and information about them is available through big job sites such as Indeed, Glassdoor, and LinkedIn. Several useful websites, including Internships.com and YouTern, focus on internship openings as well.

Skills and Personality

The work of a website developer takes concentration and patience. Anyone working independently also must have some self-marketing skills and interpersonal energy; it is a competitive field that demands a lot of customer service and the ability to listen to and understand what kind of web presence a client wants.

Technical ability also matters, and mastery of desktop publishing software packages widely used for web work is a must. Web designers code pages to format their layout, and then they apply features such as shopping carts and video to make them useful. This demands close attention to detail; a single letter or punctuation mark out of place can crash a page or an entire site. Website developers also must develop a skin thick enough to tolerate the demands and negative feedback from clients on the work they do.

On the Job

Employers

Any organization or company with an online presence needs the time and skill of website developers. Very few companies can hand off web design to employees with other job descriptions because it is a position that demands a lot of time and a very specific skill set. Tech departments at banks, hospitals, insur-

Web developers need a variety of skills and technical knowledge. They need to have expertise in programming, coding, and user interface design in addition to being knowledgeable about social media platforms.

ance companies, media companies, transportation companies, large retail stores, and real estate firms all hire web designers and administrators. Webmasters are needed by groups that have an interactive relationship with clients or customers or, like many government agencies, with the public at large.

Many relatively newer companies, such as Uber, TripAdvisor, Twitter, Spotify, and eBay operate solely via online portals or mobile apps, and the clean operation of their websites is vital to the success of the business. They are usually hiring because not only do they need a big staff of website developers, but they also have a high turnover issue since long-time employees often move to seek better-paying or more rewarding jobs at other companies.

Working Conditions

The work environment for website developers differs depending on the employer. Full-time jobs with a single employer involve fixed offices and work on desktop computer systems. Freelancers work at home on a flexible schedule set to meet the demands of clients. Long hours on a difficult project is a common experience in the field, and employers will demand overtime and weekend work if needed. Independent workers spend time developing new customers, advertising their services, talking on the phone with prospects, or traveling to meetings with their clients.

Earnings

According to the Bureau of Labor Statistics, website developers earned a median wage of $67,990 in 2017, with a wide range from $36,000 to $122,000. Salaries vary by employer category; tech, finance, and online retailers such as Walmart and the travel site Expedia pay more, and nonprofits and government agencies pay less. Salaries are also higher in tech centers such as California's Silicon Valley, Seattle, and New York.

Opportunities for Advancement

With experience, website developers with a permanent in-house position can move to management positions in sales, marketing, finance, or human resources. The skills demanded of web workers also provide a grounding in higher-level tech positions, such as systems administrator, security analyst, or information technology manager. The executive suites of major companies, where directors and corporate officers work, are also welcoming to those who have mastered the technical aspects of the company's business. In addition, the education sector needs website developers to pass on their knowledge to students, and many universities offer full professorships to experts in the field.

What Is the Future Outlook for Website Developers?

With millions of companies of every size seeking a presence on the Internet, the opportunities for website developers are always growing. The Bureau of Labor Statistics predicts that employment of website developers will grow by 15 percent through 2026, which is faster than average. Specialists in online retail and mobile platforms are in high demand. There is not a lot of risk to the career from automation since developers need interpersonal skills—which robots cannot provide (yet)—to deal with clients. Nor is overseas competition a problem because language and cultural barriers make managing overseas developers expensive and complicated for US employers. These aspects mean wages will rise with demand, particularly for developers who are skilled in all the key software and are multimedia experts.

Find Out More

edX
website: www.edx.org

A nonprofit founded by teachers from Harvard University and the Massachusetts Institute of Technology, edX offers free online web development courses that prepare students for work in HTML, CSS, and other web-oriented software packages as well as in popular languages, including Java, Python, PHP, and SQL. The site also provides summaries of information from certification courses from large companies.

Foundation
website: https://foundation.zurb.com

This library of web development tools offers online training courses from professionals and gives users the resources to easily create professional-looking websites. Browsing through the "Showcase" examples will give an idea of how beautiful pages are built and how scripts (snippets of code that instruct a page to perform a function) provide the building blocks.

freeCodeCamp

website: https://medium.freecodecamp.org

This blog is often consulted by website developers who are just getting into the field as well as by those looking to hone their skills and learn from peers and masters. There are free courses, blogs on web coding, and a post titled "15 Website Developer Portfolios to Inspire You" as well as links to sample portfolios and well-crafted websites.

MDN Web Docs

website: https://developer.mozilla.org

This site offers a beginner's introduction to the art and craft of building web pages. There's content and instruction on the keys to page development, including coding HTML, changing page formats with Cascading Style Sheets, and the object-oriented programming of JavaScript.

Interview with a Roboticist

Maria Gini is an internationally renowned researcher, developer, and instructor in the field of robotics. Born in Milan, Italy, she has also been active in the field of artificial intelligence and has created one of the first language interfaces for robots, a system known as POINTY, that allows programmers to more easily develop robot software. She is a professor in the College of Science and Engineering at the University of Minnesota. She discussed her career with the author via e-mail.

Q: Why did you become a roboticist?
A: I became a roboticist following a long path. I studied physics in Italy, I discovered the beginning of artificial intelligence (AI) and robotics by reading some research papers, and I wanted to learn more. I ended up going to Stanford University to work in the famous AI Lab as a postdoc (postdoctoral researcher). At the time there were only a few universities in the world that had robots and were using them in research. At Stanford I absorbed all the knowledge I could get and worked in the AI Lab to develop a new software tool to make it easier to program the Stanford robots. The enthusiasm at the Stanford AI Lab for breaking new ground was so contagious, I could not see myself doing anything else for the rest of my life. I am still doing it, still with the same excitement and desire to share it with others so they can also experience it.

Q: Can you describe your typical workday?
A: Each day is different, but for most of them I spend time teaching, preparing for my classes, meeting with my graduate students

to talk and share ideas about their research projects, reading new articles to keep up with advances in my field of research, and, of course, answering e-mail from students and colleagues and attending meetings.

Q: What do you like most about your job?

A: I like the freedom I have to decide what research problem I want to study, and I like teaching and working with students at all levels, from undergraduate to PhD candidates, as well as some high school students who are also working on research projects.

Q: What do you like least about your job?

A: Working in a large organization, like a public university, requires spending a lot of time in meetings, to make decisions on things such as new courses to offer, curriculum requirements, policies, and more. Meetings are important to share the governance of the organization, but they take time away from research and from working with students.

Q: What personal qualities do you find most valuable for this type of work?

A: I am a computer scientist working on robotics. Computer scientists need to be able to understand how any problem can be solved by decomposing it into simpler parts and seeing which parts can be reused to solve other problems. It is important to be patient when looking for errors in programs, systematic and organized, and capable of logical reasoning. It is also important to be creative, to come up with new ideas to solve problems.

Q: What is the best way to prepare for this type of job?

A: In college, studying computer science or engineering (mechanical, computer, or electrical) is the start. Some colleges offer robotics degrees, which combine parts of different undergraduate degrees. Working with real robots is also essential because practical experience is invaluable. Getting a graduate degree, such as a master's or a PhD, opens more opportunities, in particular for work in research or research and development groups.

Q: What other advice do you have for students who might be interested in this career?
A: There are many types of jobs for computer scientists and engineers, both in the public and in the private sector. There are jobs in large and in small companies, ranging from the development of products for the consumer market to the customization of very specialized and unique devices or systems. You can also become a professor, share your knowledge with students, and invent the robots of the future.

Other Jobs in Technology

Applications architect
Audiovisual technician
Back-end developer
CAD (computer-aided design) specialist
Chief information officer
Cloud systems engineer
Computer hardware engineer
Computer systems analyst
Database administrator
Development operations engineer
Digital marketing specialist
Digital media specialist
Digital product manager
Electrical engineer
Hardware engineer

Help desk specialist
IT (information technology) manager
Manufacturing technician
Network architect
PC technician
Quality assurance engineer
SEO (search engine optimization) specialist
Site reliability engineer
Software developer
Solutions architect
Strategy manager
Systems administrator
Tech support engineer
Telecommunications specialist
Webmaster

Editor's Note: The US Department of Labor's Bureau of Labor Statistics provides information about hundreds of occupations. The agency's *Occupational Outlook Handbook* describes what these jobs entail, the work environment, education and skill requirements, pay, future outlook, and more. The *Occupational Outlook Handbook* may be accessed online at www.bls.gov/ooh.

Index

Note: Boldface page numbers
  indicate illustrations.

Allabarton, Rosie, 66
Amazon, 28
Amazon Web Services (AWS,
  website), 46–47
application programming
  interfaces (APIs), 40
artificial intelligence (AI) specialists
  advancement opportunities,
    61–62
  certification/licensing, 56, 59
  educational requirements, 56,
    59
  employers of, 60–61
  future job outlook, 56, 62
  information resources, 62–63
  number of jobs, 56
  role of, 56–59
  salary/earnings, 56, 61
  skills/personal qualities, 56, 60
  volunteer work/internships,
    59–60
  working conditions, 56, 61
Association for the Advancement
  of Artificial Intelligence (AAAI),
  62
autonomous vehicles (AVs), 57

Block, David, 4–5
Boucher-Vidal, Guillaume, 38
Bruckner, Tom, 4–5
Bureau of Labor Statistics (BLS),
  58, 76

on data architects, 21, 22
on data security analysts, 13
on game developers, 37
on mobile developers, 45–46
on roboticists, 29, 30
on website developers, 70, 71

Carnegie Mellon University, 27, 42
Cascading Style Sheets (CSS), 50
Cassidy, Richard, 10
Census Bureau, US, 20
Central Intelligence Agency,
  11–12
certified data management
  professional (CDMP), 19
Craig, Kyle, 42
CXL—Conversion Optimization
  Blog, 22–23
cybersecurity, spending on, 10
cybersecurity academies, 11
Cyber Student Volunteer Initiative
  (Department of Homeland
  Security), 12
cyberwarfare, 13

Dassault Systèmes, 27–28
data architects, 21
  advancement opportunities, 22
  certification/licensing, 16, 19
  educational requirements, 16,
    18–19
  employers of, 20
  future job outlook, 16, 22
  information resources, 22–23
  number of jobs, 16

role of, 16–18
salary/earnings, 16, 21–22
skills/personal qualities, 16, 20
volunteer work/internships,
   19–20
working conditions, 16, 21
data breaches, cost of, 8
DataScience Graduate-
   Programs.com (website), 23
data scientists, 58
data security analysts (DSAs)
   advancement opportunities, 13
   certification/licensing, 8, 11
   educational requirements, 8,
      10–11
   employers of, 12–13
   future job outlook, 8, 14
   information resources, 14–15
   number of jobs, 8
   role of, 8–10
   salary/earnings, 8, 13
   skills/personal qualities, 8, 12
   volunteer work/internships,
      11–12
   working conditions, 8, 13
Department of Defense, US, 28
Department of Homeland
   Security, US, 12
Dias, M. Bernadine, 26

edX (website), 71
encryption technology, 9

Federal Trade Commission (FTC),
   14
Foundation (website), 71
freeCodeCamp (blog), 72

Gamasutra (website), 39
game developers, **36**
   advancement opportunities, 38
   certification/licensing, 32, 35
   educational requirements, 32,

34–35
   employers of, 37
   future job outlook, 32, 38
   information resources, 39
   number of jobs, 32
   role of, 32–34
   salary/earnings, 32, 37–38
   skills/personal qualities, 32, 36
   volunteer work/internships,
      35–36
   working conditions, 32, 37
GameDevMap (website), 39
GameJobHunter (website), 39
GameRecruiter (website), 39
Gini, Maria, 73–75
Glassdoor (website), 21, 53
graphic designers, 32
greenmail, 9
Grimes, Roger, 9, 11

hackathons, 4–5
Hotchkies, Cameron, 42
Human Factors International, 51
hypertext markup language
   (HTML), 52, 64

IBMWatson (website), 63
ICrunchData (website), 23
IEEE Robotics and Automation
   Society (RAS), 30
Institute for the Certification of
   Computing Professionals, 19
Intel AI Academy for Students
   (website), 63
Intelligent Robotics Laboratory,
   28
International Federation of
   Robotics (IFR), 31
ITCareerFinder, 47

KDnuggets (website), 23
Kharod, Dip, 18
KrebsonSecurity (blog), 14

Lawton, Jim, 26
Leap (website), 63
Leike, Jan, 57
Levy, Yael, 49–50

Magain, Matthew, 50
Mashable (website), 33
Massachusetts Institute of
   Technology, 42, 59
Master's in Data Science Blog,
   18
Mattmann, Chris, 18
McMillan, Jeffrey, 18–19
MDN Web Docs (website), 72
mobile developers, **45**
   advancement opportunities,
      46
   certification/licensing, 40, 43
   educational requirements, 40,
      42–43
   employers of, 44–45
   future job outlook, 40, 46
   information resources, 46–47
   number of jobs, 40
   role of, 40–42
   salary/earnings, 40, 45–46
   skills/personal qualities, 40, 44
   volunteer work/internships,
      43–44
   working conditions, 40, 45
Mullich, David, 33
Musk, Elon, 61
My Life with Android (blog), 47

NASA Robotics Alliance Project
   (website), 31
network specialists, 32
New Equipment Digest (website),
   26
New York Times (newspaper), 61
New York University, 42
Nielsen Norman Group, 51
Novak, Ron, 41

Occupational Outlook Handbook
   (Bureau of Labor Statistics), 76

Parkinson, John, 17
Paysa (website), 61
physics programmers, 32
Pluralsight (website), 47
Pollard, Jeff, 65–66
Purdue University, 51

Rahimi, Ali, 57
roboticists
   advancement opportunities,
      29–30
   certification/licensing, 24, 27
   educational requirements, 24,
      26–27
   employers of, 28
   future job outlook, 24, 30
   information resources, 30–31
   interview with, 73–75
   number of jobs, 24
   role of, 24–26
   salary/earnings, 24, 29
   skills/personal qualities, 24, 28
   volunteer work/internships,
      27–28
   working conditions, 24, 29
Robotics Online (website), 31
Robotics Systems Development
   Program (Carnegie Mellon
   University), 27

San Francisco State University, 51
SANS Institute, 11
Science (magazine), 57
search engine optimization (SEO),
   66
Sloan School of Management
   (Massachusetts Institute of
   Technology), 59
South By Southwest music
   festival (SXSW), 4–5

Southern New Hampshire
   University, 51
St. Mary's University, 10
Stanford University, 43
Sutskever, Ilya, 61

technology jobs, 76
   educational requirements/
      median pay in, by occupation,
      6
Tizaoui, Sandrine, 49
Townsend, Julie, 25
Treinen, Jim, 9

University of California, Berkeley,
   42
University of Minnesota, 51
user experience (UX) designers
   advancement opportunities,
      53–54
   certification/licensing, 48, 51–52
   educational requirements, 48, 51
   employers of, 53
   future job outlook, 48, 54
   information resources, 54–55
   number of jobs, 48
   role of, 48–51
   salary/earnings, 48, 53
   skills/personal qualities, 48, 52
   volunteer work/internships, 52
   working conditions, 48, 53

User Experience Professionals
   Association (website), 54
UXBeginner (website), 55
UXMastery (website), 50, 55
UXPlanet (website), 55

version-control systems, 65
Virginia Beach Technical School,
   27

website developer, **69**
   advancement opportunities, 70
   certification/licensing, 64, 67
   educational requirements, **6**, 64,
      66–67
   employers of, 68–69
   future job outlook, 64, 70–71
   information resources, 71–72
   number of jobs, 64
   role of, 64–66
   salary/earnings, **6**, 64, 70
   skills/personal qualities, 64, 68
   volunteer work/internships,
      67–68
   working conditions, 64, 69–70
Wehner, Paul, 4–5
Weinschenk Institute, 51–52
Wombat Security Blog, 15
Woz U (website), 15

Zink, Bethanne, 64–65